Whar. ..ainforest

A Killer Food Chain

by

Sean Callery

Illustrated by Shona Grant

Thank you, Shona Grant for your lovely
drawings.
S.C.

With special thanks to our reader:
Scarlett Medley

First published in 2010 in Great Britain by
Barrington Stoke Ltd
18 Walker St, Edinburgh, EH3 7LP

www.barringtonstoke.co.uk

ISBN: 978-1-84299-771-0

Printed in Great Britain by The Charlesworth Group

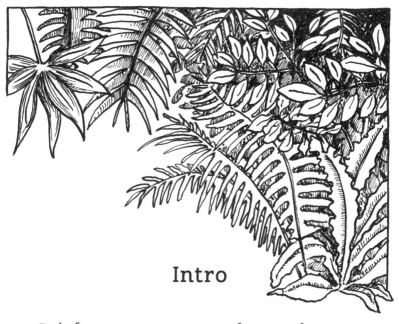

Intro

Rainforests are warm and wet. They are also called jungle.

They grow in a belt around the middle of the Earth.

It can take ten minutes for a drop of rain to land on the ground in the rainforest. This is because there are so many trees with thick leaves.

Food chains

Every living thing is part of a food chain. They always begin with a plant that has grown from a seed. Millions of animals and plants live in the rainforest, so there are many food chains. This is one of them.

Wham! Goodbye seed, hello fire ant

Fire ants eat anything. They like seeds, and will also eat worms and insects. They rip off the food and take it back to their nest.

Could they kill me?

They might kill you. Fire ants bite to get a grip on you.

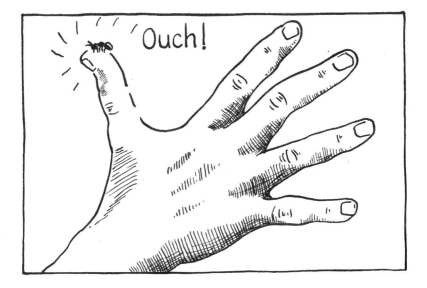

Then they use their sting. If you got stung many times by a big swarm of them you could die from the pain and shock.

Wham! Goodbye fire ant, hello poison dart frog

Poison dart frogs have bright colours and live in water and on land. They catch prey on their long, sticky tongues.

Could it kill me?

Yes. These frogs have a strong poison on their skin, which can easily kill a person. Rainforest hunters put this poison on their blow-pipe darts.

Wham! Goodbye poison dart frog, hello Amazon ground snake

The dart frog's poison will not hurt this snake. It lives in tunnels and also on the ground.

It hunts by night. It has its own venom which it uses to stun the frogs. Then it eats them whole.

Could it kill me?

No. Its venom is not so strong that it would kill a human. The snake would slide away before you even saw it.

Wham! Goodbye ground snake, hello caiman

Caimans are a kind of alligator. Most of the time they live in rivers and lakes, but will hunt on land if they have to.

Could it kill me?

Yes. A large caiman stuns with a blow from its tail. Then it pulls its victims under water to drown them. Then it eats them.

Wham! Goodbye caiman, hello jaguar

The jaguar is a wild cat. It can run fast and jump and swim well, so it can attack anything, anywhere. Jaguars live on their own in the jungle. They are hard to see because they look like the jungle.

Could it kill me?

Yes. You would not stand a chance. It would smash you to the ground and bite your skull open before you could say, "What's that?"

Wham! Goodbye jaguar, hello soil

One day the jaguar will die. Animals might eat its body or it might just rot. This will put goodness into the soil so that the seeds grow into strong plants.

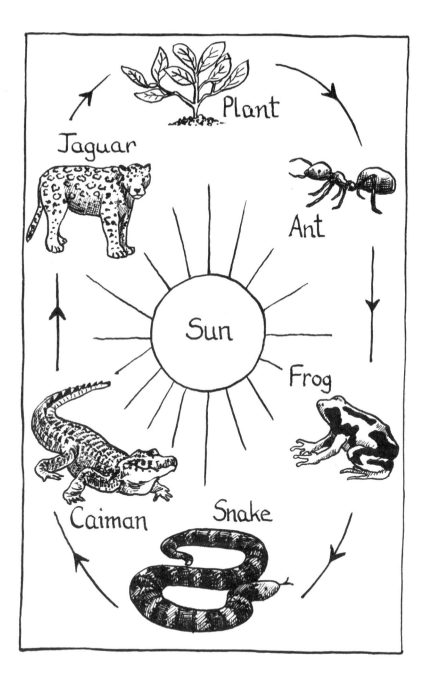

Wham! Fact file

A queen fire ant can lay 1,500 eggs every day, so their nests can get very big.

Poison dart frogs have to eat fire ants to make their venom.

Snakes do not hear well. They taste and smell the air with their tongues.

Like many Amazon animals, the caiman comes out to hunt at night.

Most cats don't like water, but the jaguar can swim very well.

WHAM!

Like this book? Why not try the others?

Wham! Arctic

Killer food chains in the freezing Arctic.

Life in the Arctic is hard. Everything has to eat —
and everything gets eaten!

From krill to polar bears, who comes out on top?

For more info check out our website:
www.barringtonstoke.co.uk

WHAM!

Watch out for more Wham! books ...

Wham! Grasslands

Life in the plains is hard. Everything has to eat – and everything gets eaten! From grasshoppers to hawks, who comes out on top?

Wham! Undersea

Life under the sea is hard. Everything has to eat – and everything gets eaten! From sea plants to sharks, who comes out on top?

For more info check out our website:
www.barringtonstoke.co.uk